# Smoke Alarms

by Lucia Raatma

**Consultant:**
Roy Marshall
State Fire Marshal of Iowa

# Bridgestone Books
an imprint of Capstone Press
Mankato, Minnesota

Bridgestone Books are published by Capstone Press
818 North Willow Street, Mankato, Minnesota 56001
http://www.capstone-press.com

*Library of Congress Cataloging-in-Publication Data*
   Smoke alarms/by Lucia Raatma.
   p. cm.—(Fire safety)
   Includes bibliographical references and index.
   Summary: Discusses the importance of having smoke alarms in the home, the
different kinds of alarms and how they work, and what to do when they sound.
   ISBN 0-7368-0196-0
   1. Fire detectors—Juvenile literature. [1. Fire detectors. 2. Fires. 3. Safety.] I. Title.
II. Series: Raatma, Lucia. Fire safety.
TH9271.R33 1999
628.9'225—dc21                                                                          98-44798
                                                                                              CIP
                                                                                               AC

**Editorial Credits**
Rebecca Glaser, editor; Timothy Halldin, cover designer and illustrator;
   Kimberly Danger, photo researcher


**Photo Credits**
David F. Clobes, cover, 6, 8, 10, 12, 16, 18
David Clobes Stock Photography/Pat Thom, 14
Gregg R. Andersen, 20
Unicorn Stock Photos/Kathi Corder, 4

# Table of Contents

The Danger of Fire . . . . . . . . . . . . . . . . . . . . . . . . 5

Loud Alarms . . . . . . . . . . . . . . . . . . . . . . . . . . . . 7

Where to Put Smoke Alarms . . . . . . . . . . . . . . . . 9

Parts of a Smoke Alarm . . . . . . . . . . . . . . . . . . 11

Smoke Alarm Batteries . . . . . . . . . . . . . . . . . . . 13

Testing Smoke Alarms . . . . . . . . . . . . . . . . . . . 15

Keeping Smoke Alarms Clean . . . . . . . . . . . . . . 17

When a Smoke Alarm Sounds . . . . . . . . . . . . . . 19

Smoke Alarms Save Lives . . . . . . . . . . . . . . . . . 21

Hands On: Test Your Smoke Alarms . . . . . . . . . . 22

Words to Know . . . . . . . . . . . . . . . . . . . . . . . . 23

Read More . . . . . . . . . . . . . . . . . . . . . . . . . . . . 24

Internet Sites . . . . . . . . . . . . . . . . . . . . . . . . . . 24

Index . . . . . . . . . . . . . . . . . . . . . . . . . . . . . . . 24

## The Danger of Fire

Smoke and flames from fire can hurt you. You must leave your home quickly if a fire starts. A fire can start and spread quickly. Smoke alarms warn you if a fire starts. The warning tells you to get out quickly.

**smoke alarm**

a machine that senses smoke and warns people by making a loud sound

5

## Loud Alarms

A smoke alarm senses smoke. Smoke
alarms make a loud noise when smoke
is in your home. This noise can wake
you if you are asleep. Ask an adult to
test the smoke alarms in your home.
Then you will know what the noise
sounds like.

## Where to Put Smoke Alarms

Most homes need more than one smoke alarm. Your home should have a smoke alarm on each level. A smoke alarm should be on the ceiling near bedrooms. All smoke alarms should be on ceilings or high on walls. Smoke rises to the ceiling when fire burns.

## Parts of a Smoke Alarm

A smoke alarm has four main parts.
A battery or electricity powers a
smoke alarm. Air and smoke enter
a smoke alarm through holes called
vents. A sensor inside an alarm senses
smoke. The horn makes a loud noise if
the sensor detects smoke.

**electricity**

power that comes into your house through wires;
electricity powers some smoke alarms.

## Smoke Alarm Batteries

Many smoke alarms use batteries for power. Remind adults to change the batteries twice a year. Adults should remove batteries only if they put in new ones. Smoke alarms without power will not sound an alarm.

## Testing Smoke Alarms

Adults should test smoke alarms once each month. Most smoke alarms have a test button. The alarm should go off when an adult presses this button. Remind an adult to test the smoke alarms in your home.

## Keeping Smoke Alarms Clean

Dirty smoke alarms might not work. Dust, grease, or bugs can block vents. Smoke alarms with blocked vents cannot sense smoke. Remind an adult to clean the smoke alarms in your home once each year.

## When a Smoke Alarm Sounds

Leave the house quickly when a smoke alarm sounds. Your home might be smoky if it is on fire. Stay low under the smoke. Follow your family's escape route. Meet your family outside.

**escape route**

a planned way to leave your home during an emergency

## Smoke Alarms Save Lives

Smoke alarms sometimes go off when there is not a fire. But always pay attention to smoke alarms. Smoke alarms can save lives. The sound of an alarm gives an early warning so you can get out quickly.

# Hands On: Test Your Smoke Alarms

Smoke alarms cannot sense smoke if they do not work. You can help an adult test smoke alarms each month.

What You Need
Smoke alarms in your home
An aerosol testing spray for smoke alarms
An adult

What You Do
1. Press the tester button on the smoke alarm. Or spray the alarm with the aerosol testing spray.
2. If the alarm sounds, you are done. Go to the next smoke alarm in your home. Repeat step 1.
3. If the alarm does not sound, make sure the power is connected or the battery is working.
4. Replace the battery if necessary.
5. Check the vents for dust, grease, or bugs.
6. Use a vacuum cleaner to clean the smoke alarm if it is dirty.
7. Test the smoke alarm again.
8. Smoke alarms can break and wear out. If a smoke alarm doesn't work, replace it with a new one. Test the new alarm to make sure it works.

# Words to Know

**battery** (BAT-uh-ree)—a small container that provides electricity; some smoke alarms need batteries for power.

**electricity** (ee-lek-TRISS-uh-tee)—power that comes to your house through wires; electricity powers some smoke alarms.

**escape route** (ess-KAPE ROOT)—a planned way to leave your home; escape routes should have two ways to leave each room and a place outside to meet your family.

**smoke alarm** (SMOHK uh-LARM)—a machine that senses smoke and warns people by making a loud sound

# Read More

**Loewen, Nancy.** *Fire Safety.* Plymouth, Minn.: Child's World, 1997.

**Raatma, Lucia.** *Home Fire Drills.* Fire Safety. Mankato, Minn.: Bridgestone Books, 1999.

# Internet Sites

**Inside a Smoke Detector**
http://www.howstuffworks.com/inside-smoke.htm
**Sparky's Home Page**
http://www.sparky.org/
**United States Fire Administration (USFA) Kids Homepage**
http://www.usfa.fema.gov/kids/

# Index

battery, 11, 13
ceiling, 9
electricity, 11
escape route, 19
fire, 5, 9, 19, 21
horn, 11

level, 9
sensor, 11
smoke, 5, 7, 9, 11, 17, 19
test, 7, 15
vents, 11, 17
warning, 5, 21